LIFE SENTENCES

Freeing Black Relationships

LIFE SENTENCES

Freeing Black Relationships

Mzee Lasana Okpara

(Fred Lee Hord)

THIRD WORLD PRESS • CHICAGO, IL

Life Sentences: Freeing Black Relationships

Copyright © 1994 by Mzee Lasana Okpara

Published by Third World Press,
P.O. Box 19730, Chicago, IL 60619.

ISBN: 0-88378-146-8

Library of Congress Number: 93-60825

Cover Design and Color Separations by Angelo Williams

Cover Illustration by Gregg Spears

Manufactured in the United States

94 95 96 97 98 99   7 6 5 4 3 2 1

Contents

Introduction

As a son, lover, husband, father, uncle, surrogate father, grandfather, and lover always of the race—the hu(e)man race and all other races trying to move out from the centers of their race, I am hopelessly in love with heartbeats and soulbeats, and terribly tired of Black hearts and souls being beaten before they can join and feel more than themselves to create a new world. Our African world has been wobbled, and spins jerkily and fitfully on its side; those of us within, women and men, caromb against each other to our separate and corporate edges.

I love so many hers—mother, grandmothers, aunts, wives, sisters, daughters, surrogate daughters, and sisters everywhere whose life complexions are deeper than private faces. And so it seems horribly unfair that those of us branded Black, who lived together through midnights and nightmares without color, who worked jointly and miraculously a dream of new days acomin', now scratch each others eyes out, go for the jugular of the opposite gender, spit venom in faces softer or harder than our own, and humiliate the spirit of those we need to make new generations, laughing as we kick in the only groins of a Black tomorrow. We cannot reproduce each other without the other; we cannot reproduce ourselves. There is no future without each other. We have paid too much to not now claim the riches of a new love made in the molten of those unspeakable costs of body and soul. We were taken together. With the immeasurable power of an unprecedented painful understanding of separations lasting lifetimes, we must come together again.

These poems, then, are from the heart to the soul, from the soul to the heart. Shot from our quiver, they are a plea for us to free ourselves. We have been hurt to the heart, and have sentenced each other out of our lives. Let some freedom rites begin with these flawed offerings, sacrifices of caked and running blood to the return of our matchless desire.

Life Sentences

I cried
and you kicked;
you cried
and I ran tongue
over jagged teeth,
filing for the kill.

Africa, white beginning.
Our trial
their trailings
our sentencing
their chains.
Parting waters.

Iron,
which we freed first
was shaped to bend us,
to lock us in linear looplets,
to leave us flat alone,
yet we kept the circle,
generations short of breath
feeling the pulse to be free.

Our eyes were soft orbits,
touches gentle;
we wept for each other
more than ourselves.
Standing straight,
we surrounded spaces of love.

We faced our custody
in each other's arms,
unborn children stirring us
with promises of their deeds.
We laughed at light bars
that held our silhouettes.

Life sentences.

New generations felt closed
by windows in supple stone
open to diamond catacombs,
seeing without our caked blood.

We had fenced them less
with old stories,
yet turning their eyes
they found freedom in black cells,
laughing at gates on all sides
before the bounties.

Then,
crooked fingers became the key,
invitations of feasts, leisure, and panoply.
They wanted,
their bellies were full of empty;
they wanted,
their backs and necks were broken;
they wanted,
love seemed shabby,
too hard to dress up.

We no longer struggle together.
We no longer lie
to get up and fight.
We want to be.
We want to be them.
We want to be free
of the fragment lines
that crisscross
small wedged openings.

Life sentences.

Although
we know the heave of breathing
is not the rhythm of soul,
that the spirit is safe
from ghoully power and disease,
that final entrapment means
our consent to be shut in,
most arise unfaithfully,
turning our backs on,
turning our backs to
the love we made
against the wall.

The living rest
must right our freedom,
living love songs,
returning home
with African spirit
without blame or anger
to the eyes and hands
that held us best,
writing new sweet blues
to keep us one.

Dueing Time

Prize Apart

These last few years,
our sisters' cries
of life and love without us
have turned my ear inside.

And I have reckoned why
we spit in each other's eye
or walk politely new poles apart,
too nice to mar the race in light.

We have suffered and prospered to forgetting.
The griot is silent in such haze,
and we cannot hear above the din
of imputation and promised praise.

Recompense

There are sins white as death
and almost as long,
violations of the head and heart
and the tearing of our limbs,

when we pulled at the pantlegs
of the monsters who trampled the earth

in order to sit on you.

Claiming last names and last words,
first sons and (hy)mens,
we have boasted of our crimes
as the sign of health.

We come now in the only time
with fists empty of splintering,
with silence and ears in our bones
to beg some eye of concern
that you have kept covered
in our assault.

Your late screams and faint rememberings
have wrestled us from the muscling nightmare,
the dream of the left side of God,
the required crawling to the throne.

We come on our knees,
having forgotten the balance of erection,
willing to work new terms
to wait the shaking of the hands.

We do not need to feel tall again,
but shall find a way to stand with you.

The He'll of My Dancing Dust

Black is forever.
In the grip of ancestors,
you learn how to live in it,
how to breathe back the flames far enough
to lick and bless the fire.

I stoked the heat
with eyes and passionate speech.
I straightened the curves I love,
angling what was round and sacred.

I did not blame myself at first.
It was the movement of wondrous globes,
the rhythms of their circularities that enchanted,
that spelled my spellboundedness.

When coupled with hot frontal worlds
that gazed back,
I forgot the ancient Egyptian warning
the picture in the river
may tell on you
without your best self.

And although it was joining
that I craved,
I multiplied them,
dividing too much soul in pools.

Not claiming love when lying,
I yet subjected all spirits
to object in consenting,
and so I burned for years.

I kept shrinking
even as I reduced faces
who proudly filed to unmarked places
to be filled and emptied again.

The flint of such fleshings
blew and banked a smoldering
that soon leaped
to scorch my eyes
and leave only
the charred spaces of my desire
to see all women through,

Then I met you,
too late to reclaim clear sight.
Each time, I watched you
through the eyes of what you felt,
I caught reflections of the spirallings,
heard the whisperings and moanings
of missing meaning.

Each sweet softness I had known
baked stone now or turned to ashes;
I saw you only through the fire.

We separate,
slipping away
on muddy banks we have poured,
parched inside.

It is he'll,
a self-made construction;
black streetcorner icon,
soul lost in the flesh
I thought my own.

Sick and Tired of this Mesh

I think I have known
for some time now
in the forty years of wandering
trying to make women my home,

I think I have known
in the first of my groin
I could not hammer out loins
and be at peace with them.

I think, I think I have known
that the semen from my eyes
may melt in several bones
but leave me all alone.

I am not a woman
so can never know
or remember the pod,
nine months of feeling God.

I buck and whinny
heave and start
in the twinkling of an heaven
which spends me back to earth,

and even when I wear
pure vestments of the mind,
I find my testicles in hand
and am pocketed from my love.

What can I do in my hungering
to keep the humping in this pit,
to savor the stretched outfit
of being two places at one?

I am African and man,
reared twice at once in this land,
set on the knees of ancient times,
spread on my knees to ride the myth.

I am over tired of this,
and need a kiss to keep past lips
to clutch the touch through work days
and at least two changings of the season.

Wish I Were Your Perfect Rhyme

I must leave.
I am not man enough to stay.
I need back what I gave away
before I loved you in your mountains.

My strength
I shot and dribbled down canyons.
My hair is gone.
I cannot push the pillar up.

I need you to cuddle my head
till my stubble curls grow strong,
and I shall be afraid if you leave me long
till I see my muscle in your eyes.

I wonder if someone had shown,
when I first opened curlilocks and yellow face
to make the heart of a woman race,
that tallies slice inside when you mark the wall,

if I might still have pushed full steam ahead,
or if instead I would have raised my sites
to where loving makes triphammering right,
and keep the ripple in my mind.

I do not know,
but maybe the question in my eyes
when little black boys discussed their lies
left me prone to too many ans(hers),

for in the center of my laugh I found a poem
and in the pupil of my tears, I found a poem,
but the brine ran down to purse the lips
that I forced open jaggedly for your kiss.

I want to be a poem with you.
Perhaps if I had not given spring of my rhyme
to young sticky snows in summertime,
I might rise and fall with you in cadence.

Middle Class Black Man

Yesterday,
I was blue
and you were putatively
in the pink
because I supported you
on the pedestal.

Day before,
we stayed in the red
for being black
to white slaves
who could not level,
much less lift their eyes.

Today,
I should know better twice
than to act male or white,
for I have lived with you
under the heel
squirming for soft, not steel.

Yet sometimes,
as you may find with child,
this world that teaches up and down
and not around
tempts you to the top
to keep from falling off.

Tonight,
help me prepare for dawn
by pressing my muscle down,
meshing sinew with soul.
I want strength to be gentle,
be tough enough to share.

Small Town Links

It was simple at first.

You and I,
woman and man,
black and black,
old enough to know how to act
would mock the loneliness
of this small white town.

That was all.

We would honor ancient forces,
wink at the seasons,
handling our own green and heat,
and talk about black writers
when the pulse cooled.

We would be friends too,
not just in the month's red edges
or the gray of distance,
but be the other ear.

We would shake hands
in our fire.

But somehow
in the celebration
of sharing this space,
in free laughter about the luck of it,
in the exuberance of new arms that fit,
even in the quieting of old echoes,

we forgot the mystery,
that same and other side of magic,
the strange counting of feeling,
that touching may not reach love
but is never plain.

Everybody grown knows these things.

Our first fight
should have opened us,
roughed up our satin hands,
leaving our whisperings more precious.

The first slammed door
should have cracked our dream,
or the telephone clicks
left longer silences.

Our droughts,
when tears were not enough
for me to grow
or even your earth to plant me
should have meant
winters too long for spring.

But we played misty,
gloved our hands,
and screamed four letter words
above the din.

We even brought wine
to water the soil,
adding apologetic gifts of black writers.

Last night was plain again.
Let us be the stars
that were not there
to see that it is over,
to ask if it ever began.
Let us settle for whatever poems
the small town links have allowed
and choose our freedom.

Tough Losses

Black men cry too.

For seven years I have watched you,
unlucky lover,
too black to let day light in
when dark was our peoples' way to win.

Your fists were too tight
for anything but soft to seep out;
you held enemies with the smile
that kept us standing.

"I am the shock troops."
You mixed that favorite line
with visions of my words advancing
after you took the ground.

The air sometimes needs pounding
when it is too thick to breathe,
and your palms out closed
might have protected you for a while.

But you wanted to knock down
and pick up with one hand
in the same motion. With the other,
you tied heart behind your back.

Black men cry too.

We lose women.
We lose jobs.
We lose appendages.
We lose the wild of voice.

The heart does not beat right
with these skippings,
but strength is to laugh
and cry at such irregularities.

Talk to slave husbands
about the awful crowd of three.
Listen to sharecropper questions
about account in loved one's eyes.

Sit on stone with old urban fighters
who lost precious smiles in fickle machines,
or on ice with hands that speak
their uselessness, losing soft fingers.

It did not start with you.
It is not just that we lose when we try.
Black fists do not hide power well
enough to escape the metal.

I have cried too,
at the back of a woman,
in front of her questions,
near her sleeping side.

I know tough losses.

Sometimes, I speak callouses.

I am not ashamed to cry for you.

I shall cry with you only long enough
to talk you back
into taking on the world again.

Coming Off a High

I don't need tables anymore
for my hands to rule,
nor a throne of sky for my head,
nor double my laughter
to double my fun,

nor my eyes doubling their centers
to expand the world,
nor sweat that changes heat
when I'm alone.

I need to reach straight for you
to build the power of our trembling.
I need to feel earth
under the toes, balls, heels of my feet
while I help seek our stars.

I need pieces of quiet
to fit our laughter.
I need to point my eyes at yours
to share the point of ours
as we keep the waters of our love
warm forever.

As Tall as a Man

Perhaps I'm growing.

For long moments, I stunted myself,
because I saw myself as short,
using the single eye
of old young cut down black men

who turned from African measures of men,
learning such dimensions were not tall
in the new world, and were shown no way
that standing straight would lend stature.

I was a giant in the new world
but saw my height as dwarf.
Money is paper, after all,
and many stand out who crawl.

So I turned to brothers on the block
before close enough to see their size,
and learned secrets, laughing and loud,
of keeping your heads in the clouds.

Some wisdom frightened me, though:
potions to make your bass grow,
piercing your arm for muscle,
eating powder through the nose;

and I did not understand the wobble,
nor sleeping in the broad of day,
nor seeing only some forever
that left friends up close far away.

Yet women looked ripe in that world,
and the men had picked them all,
and magic stories on magic corners
were jeers at failure and feeling small.

Trying to forget mother and two sisters
and the man of cloth whose words of girls
were steel sermons in my room,
I joined that tiptoe flexing world.

I sprang up overnight,

old pencil marks
on kitchen door casing
at the top of my straining head
now just bad memories.

I backed to inner mirrors though

for a big boy while
in this new measuring,
and looked instead through
the smiles of women looking up.

But the man who was polished glass
became a clear wall everywhere,
and I could not grow past tot,
with each new pair of arms propping me up.

"Treat her like she was your sister"
was the real ruler over my head,
and I could no longer shrink
beneath his favorite sermon and proud eyes.

Airlines: To a Black Stewardess

The images crowded in your form
and led you up the cabin aisle.

Face of dreams, eyes to keep you awake,
perfect teeth to nibble your tongue,
hair to towel you dry,
and a smile to swallow the girl back home.

Wound-up dolls fleshing in the air,
legs spread for nasty heights
squeezing you down to size below
or in a quiet corner of the sky.

Then you turned and locked me in
with one look and tug of your small hands,
and I could not catch my breath
or find a way to take my head
out of the clouds with you.

For your eyes held no three letter answers
nor your smile a promise to give me ground,
and I knew a night was not enough
to make room enough to share.

Out of the color they require,
you wear more gracefully your own.
You seem comfortable in black,
able to work without white aprons,
a lovely host for our history.

But,
I listen to your turbulence,
how some flights have forced you down,
how each time you wait longer
to try your wings again,
and I wonder when or if
you will work to fly with me.

I, too, have ridden troublesome air
and sought the land
to fill the pockets of my life,
but I cannot get to love on time
by advancing sure steps alone.

I shall risk new space with you
and chart its course inside;

keep your wings,
but let me cover your heart.

Definitions

Pants and skirts,
inverted triangles and curves;
such are the definitions.

Pink and blue,
tears and sinew,
such are the definitions.

Although my pants do not need the belt,
and my soul is cinched soft by suffering,
and I don pink shirts with black bottoms,
and cry so easily at muscling,

I know how these designs murder.

Yet add the mix
of American man and manners
to Othello, who is also Caliban,
and African love seems buried.

A man is what he amounts to
and what he mounts.
Measure his manhood by the size
of his mansion, meals, and meanness
and the tenderness he straddles.

And if he is black
and boy till death
yet not the old boy,
and can climb on no heads
to build his mansion
or see his meals,
he is no count.

If that does not sour him enough
to tuck his head between his legs and walk,
boasting of that contortion,
he may also watch his eyes hate
and betray the African in his face
he finds in mirrors under him.

This poem is
for the woman whose horizontal gaze
is a bridge for our understanding,
who wears pants
where my skills are short skirts,
and stands an erect soldier,
putting strong shoulders to our wheel,
whose blues make mine pastel,
yet lend large daring to my spirit.

After the Tears, Our Years

Although I weep with you
about the lack of us,
the more than many men who turn
numbers back on heels,

who, full of poison,
fill prisons with barrels in their back,
or turn their backs
for sisters and daughters of the guardians

or the back alleys of boys,
mixing guns in large death ways;
or who spin Sam's ransomed steel
to kill their reflections in the world;

although I break down
at your funerals which are our wedding,
and want to softly be a brother
until hard times are history or better,

I wince in my own brine.
Black women on the want in my wounds,
without question marks in dollar signs,
add zeroes to the sacred words;

or the salt of rivals with fair eyes,
wide hips, or jolly giants
who muscle in sweet whisperings.
Boy, you read too many books.

So, I cry with you lonely ladies
while looking through my tears
to find one of you
looking for a man who works his love.

Numbers are no measure of sweethearts
free from machines spinning the world;
those pretty African lovers who are won
by might, money, and such meridians

are no more available than brothers
behind bars, freebasing in chosen cells,
caressing calluses and codpieces,
or in other early hells.

Wherever you are,
wipe away the tears with me
and walk with clear vision
toward the sound of our union.

If you meet a man
before we reach each other,
who needs you to be strong with him
to carry more burden of our people,

who needs you to be tall with him
to see tomorrow above the burden,
and who needs you to share books with him
to piece the puzzle of your work

even as you lie and fit together,
it is still the sound of our union;
for it is a spirit that you join
and I am only one who carries it.

The numbers we must count with dry eyes
are those who love themselves enough
to love the rest of us in deed,
to multiply those figures in the future.

In an unwhimpering past,
the ancestors chose our other halves.
They do yet when we respect
the loving legacy of their labor.

Family
Reinstatement

Black Daddy

Without a model,
how could you know
but to yell at him?

With large hands
only in young dreams,
how could you remember
the soft of muscle?

Go back before his leave
to daddies who filled
the hungry smiles
of small black boys.

For life is tough
in the underbrush.
If blind heads trip your feet,
you will never be a path to manhood.

Even Your Daddy Gets Gray

You saw me before I saw you,
"cute" colored boy with curls
twisting every which way but loose.

You saw me with a rubber ball at two,
world in my small hands,
standing on a platform to be tall
in short pants and white hightop shoes.

You grew and saw the man;
shipshape fro' black as coal
closing in the face of father,
center of your robust circle

and other kids
whose daddies tapped different front doors
or stayed in dark cellars
to be safe from white bombs.

I stood on erect shoulders of history,
spine steadying bubble in the middle,
trousers too long to kneel in lint,
black combat boots in Sunday School.

But as the angle of your regard
began to shut its mouth,
you kept your own wide open
as I walked through winters
with no snow in my head
till they tied my hands behind my back
for knocking the front doors of power.

Yours had never been the house that Fred built.

Soft hands held hammers and saws
and screwed the bolts into place,
but your bellies got full
of a man with no hands;

all your eyes could see
was the table set the way of the womb,
while I dreamed and drank,
belly full before my eyes.

The color of your mother's hair
became the reflection of my lifeless hands
and the pallor in my head.

You did not know, but each night
I dyed my head to keep its color,
although dry wine washed the split ends
and new hands smudged the roots.

One desperate day
before I could seize my throwaway blade
to defend my face
from the gray it had taken on the chin,

I looked back at myself
and the black that had been
and how it still stubbled through
to frame the white
and how you three showed
no gray matter in the mind,

and I smiled first time since I was broke,
seeing no streaks at the top,
just some strands
caught in the creases of my hands.

Even your daddy gets gray.

Survival of the Fittest
(To a daughter graduating from Harvard)

To climb on heads
and walk over bodies
is no sign of strength
nor rise or line to black freedom.

It is the way of the weak
who need skulls and flesh for their feet,
who need their stamp
upon the bone and breathing of the prone.

You were not born of such spirit,
nor did the strong gentle flexing of home
tighten your muscles past passion
or bending toward the might of all.

You had the arm to wrestle Harvard,
to table his use of the purple corpse
and the jumping of the gun
to flatten the sinew of your soul.

I am proud to have been the man
to pass the power of generation to you,
the thick blood that runs unstopping,
the dream that graves could not hold.

I need you to remember that the fists
that kept me on my feet,
that fended for black folks you knew
were not too calloused to tissue your face;

to believe that the iron guts you saw rust
from the spit in my face by potentates
have been mixed to steel by salt alloys.
Yet my center is as supple as your skin.

I Mark your force, singing Laurels
as you emerge to show the fools of Darwin
that strength is the soft of love.
You have pried green from gray ivy walls.

To climb on heads
and to walk over bodies
is no sign of strength
nor rise or line to black freedom.

An Ace So Black, He's Royal
(To a son graduating from Evansville)

This town you graced at army age,
that made fodder of black boys' balls;
this place of athlete aces in forever holes,
a campus without even colored chalk

was where you would hang hat instead of head,
trading gold of your gift for white paper policy.

This butt of jokes before my grownup facts of life,
of zigzag streets and fenced in crazy people,
was where you found the bars of your blackness
the safe retreat from their wise insanity.

I knew the rope you would have to walk,
how slipping the hemp can hang you tight.

I knew how those winking lights and flashing whites
burn holes too deep for filling
while warming the skin to panting sweat
and heating the head to bottom burst.

Mark,

a man is not the sum of the eyes on him
nor his inner laughter the buy of sweet pearls;
he is as tall as what he stands up for,
and as strong as the give of his world.

How does a father explain the arith me tic
of plusses adding to nothing or even less?
The birthMark answers boys use for blanks
can never check with life solutions of men.

You did not need twenty-one for grown.
You passed the end of nerve with gentle means
of holding your mother's spirit in fingertips,
away from the aching callous of work too soon.

For you, there was no on and off the court.
The match was always now, the point the same.
You knew aces were pretty but once in a while
when the practice of your love was beyond return,

and that to toe the Mark and serve and volley
was the stuff of most games
and of which men were made.
You are made of good stuff, an ace so black
you pitch purple where royalty is in need.

Mark,

more than ever, there is a call for black kings
to softly wear their scepter and their crown
with queens who await the mix to free their own.
Then, we shall be free to cry and share the throne.

I am not of the line of deep-voiced kings
who muscle in when yielding begs for rule;
I have wanted four-fisted kingdoms to serve,
to learn the pain and glory of the natal cord.

Perhaps I would not have worn my belly in
when it was full of not providing bread,
nor crawled on all fives with a high head
if I could have earned a living in the red,

but I have seen the sole and felt its print,
and shall never need mirrors or tales again
to understand the wretched view, or retch
when life is too tight to turn over in dreams.

Though I know there are gutters you must sleep in,
I want the cold and cramp of where I've been
to be so breathing and sensate in your mind
you'll shiver and coil on high ground.

Yet when you pass skid rows, remember my spine
before the falls and the guts I made steps of
to climb back to meet your image and eyes,
and take what you can use to make your stand.

A sundown town. Evanescent sun, black boy run!
No boy, you ran over them and great white hopes.
You won against the odds. Having to pay you to win,
they add an embossed note that you read and write.

It's over now, and I, who squinted my eyes
and held my breath, stare at the black gown
they tried to scare you with, and laugh freely
as you toss the tassles to all that's right.

Continue to toe the Mark and serve and volley;
it is the stuff of life and of which men are made.
You are made of good stuff, an ace so black
you pitch purple where royalty is in need.

Spelman, Spell Woman
(To a daughter graduating from Spelman)

At the point of the slanted pyramid,
upside down in this land,
sister-brother base level
in skewed new cambridge and Ev(e)ns ville,

you are one of three wedges
into the human cracks of black souls
only a jagged line from closed;
you heal wounds as you pry.

Atlanta of the litany,
my baby in the redneck South,
unstoned head in the clouds,
Spelman, Spell Woman.

Atlanta of the Tiffany,
my baby in black bluevein South
namedropping Africa and freedom,
Spelman, Spell Woman.

Atlantis, under the see,
down under from high places
who think mountains do not breathe
and heaven is a mayor's seat.

My baby,
child Marked in her clear face,
old man T(a)rries everyplace.
Girl look like her Daddy,
Spelman, Spell Woman.

You pushed out ancient,
rounded nose and folds
needing youth to smooth,
not young enough for thin air.

You pushed out African,
high black in your yellow,
tightening Shirley Temple curls to top,
dribbling left, shooting right.

And so, my daughter
of the nighttime Mommie kiss,
of your hot kiss of Papa's cloth for Grandmommie,
of our family table bliss;

daughter, reaching back for smiles
like Satch for the high hard one,
learning the upper edges of your mouth
catch best the inside cry;

daughter, daughter, Daddy's face yet not passing,
staring at you in your mirror all alone,

his stumbling sounds cracking glass.
God! What's a basement for?

Daughter, I did not know how to jacket my arm
when it could not throw the fast ball
or even catch the ones at your head.
I thought curves would keep me a man, instead.

Oh, the fresh years in the Maryland mountains
have aired my open skin of both sides,
pulling wish and impotence to healing.
The knot is life and love.

No more turning of the key in your sleep,
doors opening now in only your wide-awake.
The white night is over,
Spell Man, Spell Man.

Never again shall I choose the question
of one space too small for us two.
I have worked in thin air to thicken our blood;
Spell Man, Spell Us.

Spelman, Spell Woman,

you always turned the heads around
and turned two eyes to one,
pushing corners to center
with the middle of your sun.

You arise lovelier than before.
Too rich for light,
you bask in the dark heat
of those who see tomorrow.

Spelman, Spell Woman.

For the Wedding You Live

Black banners do not need to be raised;
the vow to forget yourself
while remembering who you are
is African resistance to death.

The big ten and ivy leagues
are not large or green enough
to cover the airs of self
or the brown of one in the rough.

Love turned in is evol;
turned out, it is everything
we know and need to know
and all the songs we sing.

Terri and Walter,
only a you between first characters
can break this sacred bond.
Double u in we will make it better.

You two will be another beginning,
a testimony for black children's sake.
The wedding you live can save them
by being the evidence of their faith.

Wedding Promises For Keeps

Over the tongue or on the page,
words bear joyful tears and blessed fire,
seductive noises and enchanting lines,
though not enough to keep promises entire.

But rich life you rehearsed will count,
large sharing you both learned when small.
Self is at most a half, never whole;
life alone is no life at all.

So draw on kept hard-earned love
that has seen your ancestors through.
It is as abundant as racial memory;
they knew love must start with two.

The home you put up is more than dream,
stone outside, yielding love within.
Its beauty will be talk of the town,
raising faith in Blacks to build again.

Young people will watch your united place,
marvelling at splendor they note inside,
daring to fancy love castles again,
daring to believe in the lingering smiles.

Laurel and Kevin, this wedding joins you
to be what was only possible before.
Each time you share a part of life,
your love will grow all the more.

From an African Father

They have almost slipped away,
these years,
your eyes in the house.

While I would stall the stay,
inviting though your footsteps' beat,
I suffer this quarter to close,
persuaded that every dwelling
gives contour to those within.

Tomorrow,
I fancy your figures in the wind,
straight, with bow enough to bend,
so strong you need to lift another end,
moving in the rhythm of raise and reason
in the style of our first home.

You have always known who you were;
you understood all race was joined,
but black was real till color
had no power, glory, forever. Amen.

Living Freedom

To Black Women

You know you are of the dark,
whether dusk, midnight, or dawn;
you know the curl in your hair
shall be a sign for more straight worlds.

Our love is sure as the large star;
our quarrels and leavings, though real,
ash in our hands. It is already by and by;
we raise smiles from liquid guts of eyes.

Love Before Integration

We do not talk about them much;

perhaps, we do not know
our own great love stories.

Women who started sagas
of men struggling to keep one foot on shore.

Women who scurried beside their men
in dark dawns to white fields,
winking between the rows
and drops of sweat
which fell in bottomless bags.

Men who winked at their women
after watching legs pried apart
on dirt cabin floors beside clean children,
catching gushing tears,
gently turning heads around,
quieting their own red thunder.

Men who walked several countries
to find those they jumped the broom with,
taking scientific surveys of thousands
to make the point of their lives.

Women smiling with open arms,
lifting the cropped heads of husbands
returning from last accounts of freedom,
slavery for another year.

Men following north stars again,
women wearing unbought paste rings each day,
keeping their promises golden,
waiting to be sent for
with spic and span children and prayers.

Men bringing them to promised lands
to feed and clean the master's children
while they caught the dirty dribblings
of work too near the ground to be white.

Honeyed couples raising dreams together
with their children,
waiting on God, working for gold,
plying soup lines till either came.

We do not talk about them much;

perhaps, we do not know
our own great love stories.

Our Love Ain't Evol

Maybe,
if we had found a way back home
to take the famines that had come
when the earth cried open for wet
and we cried by families
with white tongues from too much sun
till we could smile as one,

maybe if we had found a way
to take the famines and plan for days
when horizontal fire would dry the water of our breath
in the blinking of an eye,

maybe
if we had known
more children of the sun past hunting grounds
formed circles too to wait for rain,
so first were last and last first,
the magic powder Europeans changed
to burst from straight lines
would have never turned us in
against our own.

But our unfamiliar fear did not wash our hands;
this land is full of those bad dreams.

Mirrors everywhere,
we had to keep looking down
to make sure the right wrists were chained
and our spirits had not devoured us.

It started there, a new way to keep from dying,
ice in Africa, cold water for drought of gun.

And on the ships,
whose moving sides were more black flesh,
they cut one band to break the rest,
and a round iron world rolled behind one foot
that pointed the way of alien sounds,
"head nigger in charge,
watch the death for your life."

And in the fields,
carpeted and square,
horizon-cornered and bare,
they struck the links of those tired of soul
and touched strange nerves
that when applied to cold
pulsed privately.

Then they taught the weary
with the history of some million years
to salute with one free hand
and take all in reach with the one still tied,
and aim bottom claw without the ball
at their high place
over our own prostrate,
while the one yet bound
was shoed to kick around
our hearted kin.

Such was the early hail and shuffle,
but it was not enough
to pit women and men.
Our new reflex was not yet sure enough
for their risking gold pyramids and swelling heads,
nor was their patting of the back
for the poking out of chest
old enough sanction
to lift dark eyes from the ground.

So they followed us to our fires,
the guarded sacred heat of hearth
that we fanned with breath and mind,
and raised their metal pryes
to burn our insides out alive,
and our love was no match sometimes
to light the lips or eyes
in the ashes of those sights
or memories.

Memory is more than clear glass;
it's a mirror too,
and we must see how looking back
means seeing through.

Black women and men,
our smooth faces wear old lines.
We cannot see behind the angry eyes
nor curve the stuck out lips
nor stop the helpless hand in mid air
not quiet the thunder of our blamings
nor open the slammed doors
shut dreams and closed rememberings
till we tuck in our feelings
and step back through the years
with the tilted head of meaning to be free.

Our LOVE ain't EVOL,
but we must return to all the mirrors
that we have been stood up to or laid before,
stand the images on their heads
and lay the reflections to rest forever,
that we may stand up inside
and lie together again.

Mirrors,
the spotless grain of the cabin floor,
showing small of back and broad back turned.

Mirrors, mirrors,
spic and span walls and waxed white tile
showing soft bone and empty hard fists at home.

Mirrors,
the streets smoothed by smooth soles
showing rough projections and tender cheeks tough.

Mirrors, mirrors,
the sparkling marble and polished porcelain
showing slumped shoulder smell of outhouse within.

Mirrors,
the scrubbed white skin and tide clean clothes
showing muscles untended and faint flex of coin.

Mirrors,
the clear concrete and washed wood
showing red too bad for blood
and dust too bleak for black.

Mirrors, mirrors,
through the rubbed tears
of quiet woman eyes and loud
and the brass cries of our slack balls and tight sack
shows the spit of the mixed cross
for ungodly years.

We must see it all back,
we must see it through
till the evol of our love
is wheeled in the real world
to become at least a kiss we can throw
toward the union of our lips forever.

For Your Questions

Your questions blare
and my shoulders slump again.

I know the origin
but my arms are too short
to raise the beaten slave from dirt sheets
where he stood horizontally.

Nor can I persuade
his living shadows
that squeezing charmin
is not the sole way
to breathe above shit
or that the best root
is not fixed
below the belt.

But I have tried to show
my sons the way ahead
by living my love for you
and reminding them that their sisters are women,
and every girl may be mother or sister too.

The boys strutting in old jockey straps
far from the slats of new baby cribs
won't stop preening in millions,
and black daughters will cry awhile yet
as they watch little worlds
lifted on big hard dreams.

But I have made the shift inside
to mix the soft and the stiff,
and I carry your eyes with me everywhere
to guard for signs of old cabin floors,
and to keep our love above dominion.

Black Axe: Cleaving for Song

Next mornings,
we butt butts while stretching,
yawning toward separate edges of dawn.

This is a ritual,
but one we must cut apart
to fit ourselves to song.

Come,
let us go back before last nights,
before our encirclements
to the round locks that mashed us
past flat turning over.

Let us repeat the promise
we whispered in blood and bile,
"we shall never forget,
we shall never forget,"

and then quicken
to the washed out fields
and the washed out faces,
to those warm snows so cold
we winked to keep our eyes open,
"we shall never forget,
we shall never forget,"

till we flesh in the last white shadows
where plaster and bleached footpaths
kept our print washable
and our knuckles the color of palms,
pointing no way to noon
where standing is without sides,
"we shall never forget,
we shall never forget."

Come this way with me
cautiously yet free
to where sealed lips probe deeper
than forked tongues,
and limbs never lattice
for positions of double crossing.

Come ! I'll come !
We are no enemies
who have to deflect our intimacy
with distance and dialect.

Roll over ! I'll roll over !
This is no trick.
I need four arms for contact
and four legs to stand.

I can't go it alone.
I need your curves to make my muscles supple.
I need your womb to rise again
in loving opposites of our same.

I still want to be free.
I have not forgotten
freedom begins in pairs,
and whatsoever I have done
in looking over you while loving you,
I shall seek to amend by looking up.

Next morning,
let us pull the sheets taut together,
leaving them dark with the clean of each other.
Our behinds have no fingers,
and those which mimic our wide mouths
can only cling to air.

Their axe with wedge blade cleaves,
and leaves close hips but separate heads.

I want you near at the inside kiss.

Revolutionary Love Music

That night,
seeing stars in my eyes
the countless time
for more than you,

you broke your clasp
to let my arms out
for the stretchless dream
of selling songs.

You knew
I wanted the music of freedom
for our people
from the quickened breath,

and from the extra paper
most see green
you knew I needed the space
to circle the enemy.

And so you watered your reluctant wish,
whispering New York,
fertilizing my hands forever.

Today,
I hustle again bold print of yellow pages,
who stand off my quickening
with standout ways.

I want to be dangerous
not for fun,
but to give my life
so I lose it,

to add a sound
so large to all souls
that only by flattening brim to brim
can they hold its harmony.

I want to sell millions
on the heart of love
so they will kiss fire lyrics
which burn old paramours.

Yet when
the wind of shut doors
sends my hands to clutch my head
to keep it on,
sometimes I break one thought
till the damp earth of your tears
pushes my roots down
and helps me bend.

Then I straighten toward circle again,
remembering our ancient need for music
was to close the spaces of silence
that beat between the people,

and believing
we are waiting on the words
to wield unforgotten rhythms,
working our freedom once more.

Words

For years I have practiced the sounds
my eyes and ears teamed to learn
when I was young,

and often I have aimed to develop
clear pictures of my mind
in the darkhouse of air
to show my inside face
to the watching thoughts of a woman.

But I have only found sufficient light
for sharp images
when I have screamed
or quietly centered my hate.

Then she saw my likeness,
but it was not worth asking for,
much less carrying around.

At least,
I needed the clicks of sweet noise
to turn out crisp
and be admired,
that I might believe again
that space could not be seen
because it was an illusion,
and so distance a production of man.

African woman,
this poem is my portrait;
and if you hold it up to your mind,
you'll glimpse an ancient spirit
smiling at you,
and you will know what I used to be
if you know yourself,
and what I want to be again.

And you will understand
that the West does not know itself,
that it is a prodigal child of ours,
whom the caves and cold made a killer,
who for its sanity had to deny
the unity of all things,
and separate language from the soul.

I will touch you in the wholeness of time,
and having already met
in the silence of this song,
our hands will take our forms,
and we shall speak as parts of each other.

Then I will never doubt
the power of Nommo again.

Beside the Movement

So often,

when my back balks in cheap contoured chair
in the chirping dark of dawn,
and I close the clean black book
continuing to mark my stare;

or when
my feet speak to straight spine
after walking three shifts of sleep
through the thick of club law in the streets
to keep awake the dream of freedom;

or when
the gravel of my voice threatens to whisper roll or stop,
and the gravel of my eyes gathers deep in my small,
slipping toward the seat front
during seventh midnight meeting that week;

I need the back of a black woman
to push against,
to sit straight with her against the foe,
enlisting armies from our history;

and want her standing next to me
against avowed and unwitting enemy
to search contrapuntal strength
in mixing of the rhythms of our feet
and two heads above the clouds;

and seek the stripped silk of her speech,
the red wise of clear eyes
to be home with me
when we have helped sharpen talk to being.

So often, afterwards,
just the small of her back in the large of my hands
would straighten forever the bend in me,
point my tottering feet ahead,
and stir the gravel of my voice and eyes

even firm

to love.

Love in Season

Anymore,
when I wonder why
love seemed late
and tapped me from behind,
I remember the nothing of never
and that I could not see
very far in front of me
till you added your eyes.

Then,
there is no need to scold time
for admitting you only
when I was grown enough to learn love.

Love is so hard to recognize
when you live black as dark,
and even when you praise the accident,
it keeps you too awake to dream.

And so,
I risk the miss and hit of language
to approach my feelings,
to explain what I can corner on the page.

You are the breath I needed for air,
the mix of bronze and deed
to stir my touch to trembling,
yet keep me searching for midnight dawn.

I love you for all the lives you love,
for the way your center never fades
yet reaches out to brush the pale with hue,
and for sweet dizziness when I stand still.

This was no late encounter,
just the tick of wheel within the wheel,
the fit of freedom and accounting,
the need of half for the round.

God is on time,
good is on time;
the rhyme of seasons is heat and cold,
not the pedometer of days.

Love is
matching the parts to whole,
using the accident of skin,
the count of sun without, within,
to begin forever with two.

Always The Fire With Us

Always the fire with us.
No need for sun or summer.
We blaze without match or earth ore.
Black bone and soul strike white heat.

After prayer in quiet pews,
or deafening pulses in bedrooms,
the look ignites the touch,
promising or fulfilling more.

And even in wooden offices
where we talk about screaming trees
that move in our trembling fingers,
leaving the moisture of years,

molten liquid wells
as we see anew the gift of nearness,
and quit gloving the pages
to print our flesh on each other.

In the unlocked streets where
we walk the direction of bloody books,
trampling old dirt echoes,
stamping new paved ways to trace,

our hands sweat as they swing,
our clothes swish cumbersome;
we sing victory in life and love
as we wait for breath to dry the flesh.

And in the required distances
that confound eye, mitt, and lip lovers,
we laugh, enlarging details of skin
we know better than our own,

touching through phones,
whispering sweet somethings of love we live,
collapsing time and space
to tomorrow and together.

Always the fire with us.
No need for sun and summer.
We blaze without match or earth ore.
Black bone and soul strike white heat.

How Could I Not Love You?

How could I not love you?

I saw you taking cracked mirrors from our children,
catch enough sun in your hands to toy their days,
rock them to rising with the love noise in your room,
and lock their knees in place with your praise.

Your straight look was a thick paddle with holes.
They took your tapers to burn their oil
and said their prayers with your syllables.

You wore the halo of their smiles.
They carried your name softly in kid titles,
bowing with straight spines and lifted eyes.

Bringing new woes and old wounds,
they watched you refuse to watch the watch,
kissing them with wisdom of happy ever after.

How could I not love you?

Holy

If we had not talked so long at first
about how to change the world,
how much there was to do,
and how close serving was to breathing;

if we had not seen the pointed fire
nor felt it blush our cheeks
when evil was the word we rode
upon the air to bridle it;

if all that unbridled passion
had not wet the sheets of feeling
before we floated down to heat
the cool white underneath;

perhaps I would not have expected
our bodies to burst in rhythm.

But we had heaved and panted
so long in love with a world to come,
trembling at the holy touch
of open arms for each other,

I knew when we closed them around ourselves,
our worlds would come together.

Nuptials

You fit in the folds of my arms,
your fingers in the spaces of mine,
but it is not that I define you,
for I set in the places of your love.

We have assumed positions of survival,
turning top and front to our side;
we are the end of grafted anger,
merging dreams of half a thousand years.

We are another beginning,
a sphinx emerging from fire before ash,
whole from the annealing heat,
head and body of one.

It is Egypt once more;
we shall show answers to save the children.
We are the reasons Africans could wait,
the evidence of their faith.

ALSO AVAILABLE FROM THIRD WORLD PRESS

Poetry:

Elvis Presley is Alive and Well and Living in Harlem
Brian Gilmore $7.95

The Present is a Dangerous Place to Live
Keorapetse Kgositsile $8.00

I've Been a Woman
Sonia Sanchez $7.95

My One Good Nerve
Ruby Dee $8.95

Geechies
Gregory Millard $5.95

Earthquakes and Sunrise Missions
Haki R. Madhubuti $8.95

Killing Memory: Seeking Ancestors
Haki R. Madhubuti $8.00

Say That The River Turns: The Impact of Gwendolyn Brooks
(Anthology)
Ed. by Haki R. Madhubuti $8.95

Octavia and Other Poems
Naomi Long Madgett $8.00

A Move Further South
Ruth Garnett $7.95

To Disembark
Gwendolyn Brooks $6.95

Near Johannesburg Boy and Other Stories
Gwendolyn Brooks $4.00

Winnie
Gwendolyn Brooks $4.00

Jiva: Telling Rites
Estella Conwill Majozo $8.00

Wings Will Not Be Broken
Darryl Holmes $8.00

Manish
Alfred Woods $8.00

Tapes:

Rise Vision Comin'
Haki R. Madhubuti $7.50

Medasi
Haki R. Madhubuti $7.50

Posters:

Gwendolyn Brooks: Celebrating A Life in Poetry $15.00